MEATY BONES

By the same author:

Inlandia (2018)

MEATY BONES

K A NELSON

RECENT
WORK
PRESS

Meaty Bones
Recent Work Press
Canberra, Australia

Copyright © K A Nelson, 2023

ISBN: 978064565163 (paperback)

A catalogue record for this
book is available from the
National Library of Australia

Cover image: Tara Leckie, *Bones of Contention,* 2021 (A sculpture
deconstructing colonialism using found objects: sheep bones and a mosaic of
broken crockery)
Cover photograph: Dominic Lorrimer
Set by Recent Work Press

recentworkpress.com

For Noni

In memory of Janet Elizabeth Millar – 1951-2022

Your mother	*My friend*
Your sister	*My confidante*
Your daughter	*My advocate*
Your aunt	*My colleague*
Your grandmother	*My conscience*
Your cousin	*My accomplice*
Your godmother	*My companion*
Your guardian	*My editor*
Your 'ex'	*My touchstone*
Your nemesis	*My solace*

Our loved one, our loss

Sovereignty has never been ceded

Three hundred and thirty seven years on
the colonial mindset shows signs
of subtle shifts, minor concessions

<u>Disclaimer:</u> the personas and views expressed in some of these poems are offensive. They reflect observations of some *types* (rather than actual persons) who have crossed my path in the last four decades. Permissions from family and friends have been obtained where they may be identifiable.Culturally sensitive material has not been shared in these poems.

Contents

PART 1

PART 2

PART 3

PART 4

PART 5

PART 1

PART 1

The peacemaker

I watched this woman walk into a battle silent and unarmed;
saw her take the weapons from her warring clan of women.
Unasked, she came to help when redback spiders overran
the building; after whirly-winds, she helped tidy up the yard.
We could not speak each other's language. Our bodies
leant towards each other in handshakes, nods and smiles.
Sometimes we sat together on her country.
Through an interpreter, she told stories, pointed out two
distant peaks as a woman's place then painted it for me.
We gathered ininti beans together. Shared food.
Arm in arm many borders frayed. That year I had
Oogeroo Noonuccal's poetry by my bedside, learnt
her poem, 'Song of Hope', by heart. I asked if it could be
translated for The Peacemaker. Once heard, she thought
'the glad tomorrow'—Oodgeroo Noonuccal's last line
in that verse—might be a first line in another song,
one for this new century.

At the single women's camp

Molly, Biddy, Addie, Bess and May don't care about the grey beards sprouting from their chins. They couldn't give a wild fig about their matted hair, old scars—they had fought and won their battles in the 1980s—their land!

They burn wood, hotwire seeds for necklaces, paint dots on canvases marking time. They're laughing at the antics of the dogs or one more whitefella who comes with questions, other kinds of wanting.

In their small circle behind this fence, they've finished mothering. They're mostly silent now and wise. Their only wish—a decent feed, a lift to country when things are ripe—wild passionfruit, bush tomatoes, ininti seeds.

Let the young ones hunt echidna and goanna.

After all their gathering, these women are content to sit, sip tea, eat what we've packed in eskies or a box. They've stopped bleeding, crying, caring, wanting anything except trips to country, ceremony.

Look!

Molly, Biddy, Addie, Bess and May are painted up! The ochre patterns on their bodies map their country. See how they gently stamp their feet and sway?

Listen!

They're singing up hills and soaks and dreaming sites with bare breasted dignity, knowing limbs, ochre lines and circles—the language of the land. Each woman's body is their country, a songline they pass on to younger women, kin.

Why I keep a digging stick under my pillow

Some men want to hurt us,
men who have the strength
and cunning to break in, sometimes
in twos, threes, whole platoons.
And sometimes, after taking
everything, these men want
to rub it in.

Even though the point of my digging
stick could penetrate flesh without effort;
the thick end may, with a minimum of fuss,
knock a man out, crack a skull, shatter bone,
this isn't the main reason I keep
a digging stick under my pillow.

                    The heft of memory
              when I touch its polished hardwood
          takes me back to a chase across rough country,
        running with women, goanna going to ground,
            women digging, dirt flying, the *whack*,
            and burning flesh, our greasy fingers ...

              Oh, the freight of dreams rumbling north
            on a two-lane highway! Swags under stars,
                the company of women around fire,
                        sparks flying ...

                How we redesign the Milky Way,
              reshape the whole bloody universe.

Desert flâneurs sequence

1.   The bureaucrat

No suit, no tie, no top hat on his head
no polished leather shoes, no brass-
handled cane—the desert flaneur
comes dressed for comfort:
short sleeved cotton shirt,
loose cotton slacks,
Akubra for a bit of shade.

He moves around the settlement,
clipboard in one hand, Mont Blanc
pen in the other, itching to tick off a list
in premium ink. There's perspiration
on his upper lip, his underarms,
perhaps his crotch …
He curses the temperature,
and his bloody awful job.

The flies, the stench, the upturned
rubbish bins (three ticks),
the feral donkey problem (tick),
the dogs, all interbred,
look full of ticks to him.
He gives that box two ticks
for emphasis.

His latest model four-wheel drive
awaits, like Charon's skiff, to sail
him out of Hades, back across
the Styx. The river's dry
and sandy here,
beyond the cattle grid.

This afternoon he'll take
his clipboard back to town,
review his list,
shower, sink a few
long necks (Full Strength),
compose a succinct
analysis for the Government,
hammer home his message.

2. The local government inspector

I fly in on the mail plane—a not unpleasant flight—
no other passengers detract, no unnecessary queries,
no bugger chundering in bags … The council clerk
is there to pick me up, take me to lunch. At the compound,
a German Shepherd the council clerk calls *Goebbels,*
is forcibly restrained. A six-foot chain link fence is,
he claims, a necessity. It keeps the local vermin out.
He likes to garden. I suspect the sprinkling system came
from the Works Department, but who am I to judge?
Lunch is salad, freshly picked, cold leftover lamb.
A pinot noir is offered and declined—this settlement
is 'dry'. We settle for a glass of aqua minerale,
a dash of lime. The inspection takes two hours.
I observe Essential Services still runs well.
The council clerk has a Good Man in charge, but
the dickhead likes to stir the Good Man up, in front
of me. That's one black mark. The Workyard's
been vandalised, again. The council clerk says, *I know
who dunnit—three little shits with nothin' better to do
but trifle with me 'ead.* I wonder if he's on medication?
The garbage tip's the clerk's pride and joy, fenced
and locked each afternoon at 5pm. He's had fun
with an excavator, dug two great bloody holes he's
proud of—one for general household rubbish, one for
animals found dead—I counted a dozen donkey carcasses
when I peered in. When asked why so many, the clerk
replied, *silly fuckers got 'emselves locked in an empty
house—you shudda smelt the smell, seen the flies. What a
shitfest. I got my 2.I.C to clean it up, then he quit,
the squeamish git.* There's a pile of metal—old car bodies,

fridges, angle iron, another labelled 'plastic' and one
for worn out tyres. All very neat, this garbage tip—
his one big tick. Pity about the settlement—it looks sick.
The council office runs like clockwork. Martha keeps a lid
on things, wears the trousers. I'm pretty sure the council
clerk slips her a bit of 'you-know-what' after working hours.
All in all he's doing fine. Not ten out of ten but maybe nine.
The local staff are satisfied, as far as I can tell. The trouble-
maker I heard from last time has relocated to the clinic where
she plays merry hell with pharmaceuticals. So *he* tells me.
Back at the airfield, I make small talk with the pilot, who seems
so young, he should be back in high school, or britches, but
he's no fool. He's getting flying hours up to move from mail planes
to ten-seaters in the Top End, come the dry. HQ should be pleased
with my report. I predict the clerk will stay on quite a while. My take
on him? Ninety-nine per cent 'mercenary', not a scrap of 'missionary',
a little bit of 'misfit' thrown in.

3.   The minister and his first assistant secretary

the minister for Aborigines may drop
into your community
if convenient—if it's not too far off
the highway, or it's near a town or city

he'll exchange pleasantries
with local dignitaries
over lunch that you provide …
that'll keep him on side

> chartered plane
> tight timeframe
> fly in fly out
> one trough, one snout

the minister may bring his right-hand man
a first assistant secretary
who only likes to fly first class
top dog at last
don't dare call him a horse's arse
or he'll make your lives a misery
with his white supremacist policies
and besides, he'll still be there long after
the minister or his ministry

4.   The carpetbagger

Behind tinted glass, in cool air, he drives a BMW 4 x 4,
playing classics. He pays no heed to passing country,
carrion, birds circling—he has one eye on the road,
the other on the *steal*. He's ready to haggle, cut a deal.
In the boot there's primed canvas, a comprehensive range
of acrylics; cash in a swollen wallet locked in the glove box
and, of course, he has his *spiel*.

The only covenants he has are with his banker and certain
matrons in the city who would die for a splash of colour
by an Emily or one of the old riverbed masters. It's simply
business, money for jam. Back in the city he has open
mouths to feed. He settles with a handshake. Before he takes
the steering wheel again, he wipes his hands with a liquid
antibacterial—it's *industrial*.

His growing caché—canvas stretched and framed, baskets
woven in the great tradition of Top End women or desert
weavers, cross-hatched barks, nicely boxed, go down well,
especially *the names*. If only he could get his hands on a few
tjuringas, he'd have it made. Back in Toorak, he moves
smoothly through the scene—from black t-shirt to black
polo neck, black Armani jacket, wrap-around Versace shades.

In that rarer cosmos—the dark web—bigger deals are made.
He celebrates gross profits. Give that man his next line of cocaine!

5.   The plumbing contractor

I can almost do the ton on this stretch
of dirt—me truck's weighed down
by tools and parts—helps me go fast.
I've got plumbin' symbols in me head,
a job list and a timeframe. This week
can't end soon enough—it's all about
sludge and scum and effluent.
Let's hope there's no catastrophic
septic scenario, a clogged or failed
drain field or I won't make it back to town
for pub and grub on Friday night.
A three-day workin' week means I can
write a five figure invoice and I'm not
talkin' cents. Blackfellas out here know
bugger all. Even though I'd rather be lyin'
on my back under a sink or in some
shiela's swag, I'll deal with their shit.
It's all money in the bank. Still, I'll exact
more leverage on these coons with my
hacksaw teeth, I'll stick 'foreign matter'
in their traps—they'll have to call me out
again. Bacteria won't be able to do its job—
make 'new colonies'—but I will. I'll screw
a gin or two while I'm here. Uppity blacks
couldn't see a blockage in a drain
even if they had a big, fat torch with l.e.d.
They wouldn't know the diff between a flat
or Phillips head, couldn't use a bloody plunger
if their lives depended on it. Why they
don't piss and shit in the bush like they used to
is beyond me, but I'm just a simple man,
here to make a quid.

Sparky

We call the Essential Services Manager, *Sparky*. He's the most important white man in this remote community, in charge of power and water. The deluded council clerk thinks *he* is first among men— bow down! Of all the whitefellas here, twenty of them, *Sparky* is my favourite.

He's no gatekeeper or gossip; no cruel tyrant spruiking dodgy theories of community development; no closet alcoholic; no Mister Plod, chasing others for minor misdemeanors; no self-styled 'somnambulist' creeping round the single women's camp at night; no preacher, either, who thinks he is the new messiah.

Most mornings we converse at my front gate. He's on the job, doing what he's paid to do—checking water quality, taking samples, using chemicals and gauges. After testing, he explains why I can drink from any local tap.

When the council clerk gets on his back or when vandals tamper with his hydrants, *Sparky* fixes things then takes a weekend break. His nemesis is water streaming in wasteful flow, and man-made power outages. When the powerhouse was broken into, he didn't go ballistic—he decamped to coastal calm. But first he met with Elders, took their advice. Reassured, the problem solved, he went on leave.

Mind you, thirty years ago and further north, two Warlpiri men ran the powerhouse. Plumbing contractors from town were the problem then.

Sorry business

Covered in white clay
Jangala welcomes the mob.
One more Elder down.

I pay my respects
in drinking water, blankets,
a kangaroo tail.

Bright blue tarpaulins
tent the river bed,
can't contain their grief.

Keening is by nature
mournful, but there is beauty
in this sad ritual.

A ceremony involving
the old man's swag
will take place today.

The messenger says
his wife wants me
to be there with them.

Strong brown arms guide me.
I watch as his possessions
are placed on his swag

gently, one by one—
mobile phone, enamel mug,
clothes, all neatly rolled

into the canvas.
The modesty of living
rough, belies his proud life.

He was a Big Man
with a large extended clan.
Fought hard for land rights,

teased me every time
he saw me—*you be right skin
for me, my next wife!*

He was a gentle
cattleman, a gentleman.
When they buried him

the council backhoe
scooped the earth until it bled
for its custodian.

Afterwards, the mound
looked like a southern mountain—
plastic blooms above

arcing like rainbows
over body, coffin, swag:
his earthly gold.

Love poem

You were a knight shining white, an escape, bright spark in dark
firmament—the job. We hummed. We hummed over bitumen and
we hummed over gravel, washouts, corrugations. Once you were
fitted with 60% tread we were Mozart's Clarinet Concerto in A, a
desert song, a lyric poem, no tantrums, smooth sailing all the way to
Yuendumu the back way after rain. I merely turned your wheels left
or right, you did the rest—avoided great expanses of bloody mud or
floated through a wall of water. We were fully engaged. You may
have slipped a little, but you gripped when it counted with a strength
I didn't have.

I'd fill your tank, check your oil, top up the air in your tyres. You
started every time. Held me comfortably. The two blowouts were not
your fault. You had spares and though the Bluetooth didn't work we
weren't short of music.

When we went to town, I'd take you to the carwash, lather you as
gently as a woman working in an Instanbul hamam—as tenderly as
that—then I'd take the pressure hose in hand, wash off the foam. And
the red mud broke off in chunks and slithered into indented drains or
broke up into what looked like clotted blood that poured out into the
Todd. You reminded me of a man in a new tuxedo after I blackened
your tyres and polished your rims.

At the Hilton, I'd park you in shade before I booked in. You waited
patiently the whole weekend. I rang for room service, had a meal from
the Hanuman, drank margaritas, and swam while you stood guard.

I might have been behind the wheel on our last drive to Alice Springs,
but I was sick and drugged and can't remember much except arriving
at the hospital. You saved my life. I owe you one.

Metamorphosis

Crow fouls my drying clothes, steals
wild passionfruit before it ripens,
spoils the air with *caw caw caw*

I curse you, crow—
little shitter, thief,
tormentor

A Warlpiri elder tells me,
your totem, crow.
My silent protest—*no, no, no!*

Now I must *protect* crow
love crow, *become* crow—
its garbage tip mentality
soaring appetite
its dogged quest
to be hated

A Napangardi I know says,
Sis, you lucky to have crow—
I'm emu. Not glamorous, like crow

As glamorous as a running sore
yesterday's road kill
meaty bones picked clean

Crow speaks. *So! You think I'm rubbish!*
Can't you see my sequinned
evening dress, my feathered stole?

Stay a little longer. I won't feast
on your carcass—I'll turn
your silly head . . .

I am crow—
the classic little black dress
is my everyday,
my eyes are not yellow
cake or coal. They're diamonds.
I sing brassy psalms
for my young—
avian and human

Both ways

After Gary Snyder's 'Back Country'

Mapping country—
take a satellite photo enlarged on primed canvas
ochre background
chalk in boundaries   waterways

we meet the old men
their wives
sisters

eat together—
corned beef oranges onions carrots
simmered in a flour drum
white rice   billy tea

the campfire   dies   down
stars   come   out

in a rundown demountable
we sleep in swags on wire beds or floors

the men sleep near the dying fire

next day work starts with *good morning*

breakfast/books/maps
other countrymen's story/book
tea-bagged cups of tea

a bit about us
where we've worked
who with

connections made/a beginning

six litre pots of acrylic paint
i-phone camera
site visit/field trip
video footage
a big story to map

gather plants
listen
categorise
dictionary work for proper language spelling
listen

the ladies work with us/tell stories/jokes
chew bark/ash/tobacco

four-wheel drive convoys—
a fenceline tracking south
foot slog to unmarked graves

listen
gather more plant samples

white crosses
plants/birds/animals emerge
in chalked outlines

one bush for smoking babies
one for treating boils
one tree gum a tea for cancer/kidney disease
bush food
bush medicine
bush lore

soak/swamp/creek/rockhole
fruitcake/apple juice
bush flies inside/out/mouth/nose/ears/scalp

a black-headed python

                              slides

                                        onto   the   canvas

five women sit around the map
small sticks dipped in white paint
dotting outlines on black images

milky tea goes cold
bush flies on rims of enamel cups/drink/drown/float

dingo tracks
the only marks I make

                    day ten … last field trip
                    distant mountain
            another convoy/another fenceline
                bush bashing north this time
                old car wreck a marker
                    for the soak
                    we couldn't find

                        my *faux pas*
            broken side-mirror/damaged door
                       no lives lost

                    shame job though

        one map—traditional country—their lease
          surrounded by three pastoral stations

                           fingers point
                    there   there   there
                        naming them

heads shake/ironic laughter

                          this time next year
            a celebration/community BBQ planned
                        map/big book
                        story of place
                        owners/managers
                        what's important
                      where we go from here

hands shake—working hands/soft city hands
brown/white

then
        farewell—

        See you on TV, I quip to the Elder, star in recent documentary
        Come 'round again, he says/waving goodbye/grinning

Bush fly plague
News from Alice Springs, April 2019

Cyclone Trevor travels inland, bringing unseasonal rain. Unseasonal
winds deliver unexpected visitors to Central Australia.

Glorious desert sunrise
we cannot enjoy—
bush fly plague

            Dawn walk—
            she uses a switch
            to stave off early risers

                        Seeking moisture
                        a dozen bush flies
                        drown in my tea

Old saying, *a flea
in your ear,* takes on new meaning—
bush fly!

                sixteen bush flies
                swallowed—she learns
                to shut her mouth

Bush fly plague—
Buddhist teachings
out the window

Door ajar—another hoard
of bush flies come in
uninvited

Fly swats—
no match for
bush flies

Mortein—no defence
against this plague.
More likely kill us!

The women complain—
These flies landing on my tucker!
Still they eat

She sits perfectly still
for a photo, bush flies crawling
over her face

The dog competes
for his dinner—
bush flies win

Haven for bush flies—
her thinning hair,
sweaty scalp

A strong south-easterly
comes through—still
the bush flies hover

Fly veil—
no panacea against
bush flies

Bush bashing—windows up
aircon on high—bush flies and humans
bump along together

Finger on one nostril
she snorts snot out the other—
bush flies in the stream

Tissues held over her mouth
she speaks—
toomusbusflytoday

She attempts to compose
a Terms of Reference
fly swat by her side

she taps on the computer
puffing out one side of her mouth—
wards off bush flies

Plumber quits repairs—
Too many bush flies!
Both problems persist

Bush flies drown
in paint pot
stick to the wet canvas

Our meal—
good stew, rice
peppered with bush flies

The finished canvas—
dead bush flies
immortalised in paint

Bush fly plague—
where are dung beetles
when needed?

Swat, spray, switch—
nothing beats bush flies
except the sun's disappearance

After dark
bush flies sleep—
moths circle the light

Barkindji Guide

1

On flat country, near the sick river
you lead us to a cave
through rocky, snake-infested terrain.

We mount a steel platform.

A white line—silicone—encircles rock art.
Someone, scientist or poet, says: *It prevents*
the rain gods weeping their tears of erasure
on ancient treasure. White ochre men dance
with women, emus, fish, kangaroos; you point
to cadmium coloured figures—warriors—
like dwarfs beside life-sized stencilled hands.
Your voice fades. Time stops   images catch
in black, dilated pupils,
fish trapped in stone.

2

You know more than you're telling: a history kept
from us—massacres covered up, unmarked graves;
unprotected sacred sites.

3

At a picnic lunch, we make small talk.
Once I had the perfect job, you say,
caring for country, fortnightly pay—
denied leave, PTSD.

Nothing can help you forget
what your grandfather told you—
Nothing can help you unsee the semi
trailer running over young cousins—

not all the rock art here,
small town racism,
medication in the world.

4

In the Bowlo that night, we share a Chinese Banquet.
You play a video clip kept on your i-phone—
a scientist reassembling bones, a skeleton found
in a flood-eroded river bank after rain.
Only one bone missing.
Forensics confirms the twenty-year old male
died from axe wounds to the head.
Your aunties found these bones.
After rain, my grandfather found gold.

5
Tomorrow, you have an appointment
at the abattoir—semi-permanent job
cutting throats, skinning livestock,
bucketing guts.

6

Over vanilla ice cream, nuts, flavouring
we talk the lingo of PTSD, yours and my
brother's. *Fourteen drugs, still my brother*
drops his bundle.

All the traumas in the world,
right here in our backyard.

7

You're saving up to get an ABN, become
a tour guide. I ask how much you'd charge.
$120 a day, you say and I butt in—
Consider your cultural knowledge.
Think about administration on-costs,
insurance, superannuation …
it's got to be more like
$1000 a day.

You look at me and grin.

A review of Henry Lawson's legacy

The Barkindji poet's mouth,
so close to mine, spits
the 's' in 'Henry Lawson'
onto my left cheek;
when the word 'hate' explodes
from his lips into my left ear,
it exits my right
like a rumour.

He has presented a paper at a Readers Festival
in my hometown—a small-minded municipality
I escaped in my teens—a place where the famous
bush poet grew up; a place where today's
inhabitants (suckled on hero-worship)
recite what five generations
(convicts and settlers all)
including me,
have done before them.

He has walked in a street, a park, beside a creek
named 'Lawson'. It irks. Worse, a member
of the audience has asked, *how many
wives do you have?*

I want to run …

What offends him more—how Lawson vilified
his people—*harsh, harsh words*—or left them out;
how the bush poet never bothered to learn

the Darling River's Barkindji name, like
so many other old white men then,
like so many others today.

I feel the weight of his pain—the burden of his lived
experience in this country we now call Australia.
I place my hands on the shoulders of his slight
frame—fragile vessel—that has taken
so many beatings in New South Wales
police stations ...

Brother, you've got to remember
Lawson died a penniless,
lonely, alcoholic ...

You've got to remember
to write your own poems.

The master key

There are two hundred people in this community.
I'm the one with the master key
to the newest building,
the staff houses.

When I walk from the office to the Hilux,
the keys around my neck
rattle on my chest
like medals.

In the past I have criticised the men—
those old white men—in charge,
who told the locals
to call them 'masta'.

Now I feel like one of them ...

Checklist for future interventions

After Tess Lea's 'Wild Policy'

Act on a political opportunity, seize on a scandal
Remove legal impediments
Seek bipartisan support for new policies
Engage a communications specialist

Handpick a sympathetic Chief Executive Officer
Override impediments and naysayers
Lampoon any opposition
Escalate the problem
Schedule urgent briefings with key APS staff

Hold a press conference
Outsource non-critical functions
Lease buildings and install temporary offices
Dictate information flow

Utilise a (white) workforce who are willing to
Strategise and operationalise the intervention

Market the appearance of institutional coherence
Undermine Aboriginal dissent
Grasp the nettle; uproot it
Signpost a significant budget (tied to concessions)

Tender for multiple whiteboards and Post-it notes
Overlay policies in new administrative language (and acronyms)

Reconfigure reporting trees to increase the look of probity
Amend the rhetoric when KPIs flag
Neutralise risks, leaks and unruly personnel
Shroud negative reviews and audits
Order a 'lessons learnt' approach
Minimise fallout when outcomes fail to materialise
Embed records in vaults and archives

(Study freedom of information legislation
Impede access—shred documents
Create a policy shift)

PART 2

PART 2

Toxic masculinity in three acts

For Jo Dyer (and Kate)

Act I

Wine. More wine.

He takes my naïve hand,
leads me to the circus ring.
Pointing to the high trapeze
he says, I want to share my
expertise with you.
He removes the sequinned
leotard he normally wears,
whispers 'swing'
and 'trust me'.

I do.

Instead of tandem flying,
I fall. He pushes my nose into
piss-laden straw. In that bent
position he performs an act
so lewd I cannot name it.
Then he drops me.

Broken and ashamed,
condemned to silence,
I crawl and don't stop
crawling until I pay—
for psychotherapy.

Act II

Meanwhile, he flies
from Big Top to Big Top,
ascending every ladder
placed within his reach,
he performs each new act
with adroit precision.

He is just one step
removed from the top
position in The Greatest
Show on Earth (in Australia)
in the opinion of those
in bed with Power
and Ambition.

Act III

Enter jugglers, acrobats and clowns,
stunt men, trick ponies, hams,
fire breathers performing in three rings.

Three ringmasters—politician, journalist,
and judge—use whips and megaphones
to choreograph the drama,
keep it moving ...

The audience at large is quite delighted.

Sex and Death—
two great themes—
play out.

Drumroll … the music sounds a lot like
Wagner.

Acts of contortion
stilt walking
can go awry

looks awkward
no matter
how well done.

The curious will always love a freak show;
will want to watch a strongman or a sword swallower
err as he tries to make a killing.

No matter, when reputations end in tatters, sideshows
draw a dwindling crowd.

Still, the rolling globe rolls on.

Sleuth

Acting on intuition, following lines of inquiry, she bagged clues, went forensic and gathered dead skin cells, semen, spittle. Phone call records made shitfuckery of orphaned words, confirmed critical lies, gave up names. The bodies were found scattered across three city suburbs. One key witness spilled the beans—dates, times, places, alibies—a counter narrative to his spiel.

The Big Reveal released duped women from a gifted liar's thrall, something any Dickless Tracy could be proud of.

Curse and plea invective

After reading Catullus (c 84–c 54 BC) at the
Rome, City and Empire Exhibition, National Museum of Australia, 2018

Placing a marble hand on my stony heart
I invoke a blank-eyed curse:
You, who snatched my virginity with so little sensitivity—
a pox on you and your Bondi Penthouse; your Gold Coast
Condominium; the million acre property you call 'Felix Australis',
where Limousin bulls inseminate Angus cows for good meat and profit.
May a corrupt manager pick, pickle and steal your olives,
crush your exotic grapes with filthy feet, bottle your grand crus
and drink the best of the Brunello, diminishing the tax breaks you are
Oh So Aware of—may he fuck-face and sodomise you over and over,
you gaping asshole of a donkey.

Mercury, hear my plea:
send ten thousand fleas into the minotaur's
jocks, let him scratch until
his balls fall off.
Your faithful servant,

Europa

Advice from a Greek god

Turning the desk calendar this morning
I thought of you—the message
from Chronos read:

> *You cannot make a sparrow hawk*
> *out of a buzzard*

Blocking you
makes perfect sense

Scale

It was not
on the same scale
as *Depp vs Heard,*
but he took her name

to a small town,

a smaller circle,

where he rearranged

all the letters

into one word—
vindictive

The other woman

had one word

for him. She found

it in the DSM—
narcissist

Housekeeping

After Nikki Giovanni

He would visit her on weekends.
Within half an hour of his arrival,
he would sit in one corner of her tidy

living room, dressed only in his underpants
smoking non-filter Camel cigarettes. Ash fell
on the polished floor. Empty beer bottles

lined up like skittles around the legs
of the armchair. She had given up smoking
by then, but had not given up having

sex with him. That came later, after
she tired of his constant refusal to stop
chewing tobacco without a spittoon.

One small step for a man, a giant leap for me

The moon reminisces

After a panoramic sweep of my surface
he propelled his capsule toward me
sent out a probe, adjusted his approach.

Our metabolic rates rocketed.
He had difficulties squeezing through
the hatch. It opened at 02:39:33.

He performed manoeuvres, planted
his flag, landed in the Sea of Tranquillity
proclaimed it a magnificent desolation.

Peri menopause

After 'Fake' by Stephanie Wood

Before the first lie is exposed,
suspicion heralds the end.
If suspicion is not confirmed,
you become a yo-yo in his hand,
a *sleeper*, condemned to travelling
around the world at his whim,
walking the dog (his), unravelling
in slow motion.

So she phones the gallery, impersonates his sister. She wants
to give him a gift—a subscription—asks if he has one current
or not. The helpful assistant affirms a recent renewal—
another two years.

To be certain, she spells his surname, asks if his 'partner'
(the one he said he'd separated from five years earlier),
is also named on the subscription.

Yes.

She presses the 'end-call' button of the i-phone,
this truth her new reality—
one lie means many.

That night an irregular menstrual flow begins,
a heavier bleed than usual,
the last she will ever have.

Another litany

With thanks to Billy Collins and Jacques Crickillon

I am the hot coal, the leaping flame
in the fireplace, the sound of rain on the roof ...

I also happen to be the pure wool rug,
not your cold tiles or acrylic carpet.

And a glance at these walls will confirm
I am the landscape above the piano

with the pink and green rocks, its orange
hill and blue riverbed. You may qualify

as the compost, but you are *not* the mauve
irises, pink violets or red geraniums. I am.

I am also the orchid, the daphne, the jonquil.
I also happen to be the Chanel No. 5,

whereas you are the empty bottle of Old
Spice, the horny goat-weed capsules

in your man-bag, the self-help books
on the floor of your shiny sedan. For your

information, I am also the knife. You will
always be the bread. Even if you were

the sponge cake, you would be stale, like
the bread. As for the crystal goblet

and wine … let's talk instead
of champagne flutes, a sparkling

vintage chardonnay. Let's toast my survival
after shedding light on your infamy.

No escape

Beware the invisible Angry Older Women: you won't see us coming.
(Ingrid Banwell, smh.com.au, 9 January 2023, 5am)

You may think

you have escaped

with the deftness

of a fly, but

remember, I am

a dab hand

with a swat.

Three small anti-love poems

Warning signs: the hair dryer
he used on damp sheets
after making love

Next to his toothbrush—
Dr Tung's stainless steel
tongue scraper

6.9 on the Richter scale—
his lies—*I want monogamy,
etcetera, etcetera*

PART 3

PART 3

Three small love poems

Lovers, early morning—
How long have we got?
Oh, about thirty years ...

Music to make love by—
'War of the Worlds'
or 'Bolero'?

Who sends pinecones
through Australia Post?
A lover expecting fire!

Yanyuwa love songs

Beneath the stars in bush at Borroloola, women sing the man to me—songs as ancient as the land, a gentle tempo, a language I don't understand.

My grandmother, Yanyuwa way, tapes the women singing. When it ends she hands the tape to me. *Take this with you. Play it. He will come.*

He came.

He went.

A daughter born,
a father gone, still—
a happy mother

You asked about the circumstances leading to your birth

We exist only by chance. Plans go awry, are misplaced or forgotten.
Often, there is no plan, but in your case I measured the movement
of the moon, calculated—no, counted on—knowledge and desire . . .

I supposed such calculations might misfire, thought your chances
slim—old seed, dry ground—but I believed in poetry, blood, the magic
of particles and a spirit of equivalence.

At a time I knew favoured the feminine,
failure, unintended consequences
seemed probable.

But what else mattered?

Cautionary thoughts—
career, cash flow, reputation or convention—
almost unmade us.

I did not heed them.

Almost dreaming, acting alone, something deeper played out,
something primal, something *mother-in-me* perhaps ... call it instinct
or longing or precious time passing.

Call it payback if you're inclined—quivering bottom lip, small bruised
heart, memories of men, unholy ghosts, their shrouds piling up
smothering possibility—or the mess inside my head.

It may have been as complex as a wish to return to a mother's bed, breast, womb; as uncomplicated as the desire to bond for life with another female made in my image, entirely herself.

Memento

You came to stay seven years after we parted.
I cut my finger scoring a shoulder of lamb

while you met an old friend at a nearby hotel.
After dinner, you slept soundly by my side

in the only double bed, as I breastfed my six-month
old baby, the baby we could have had together,

if only …

After you left, the wound became infected,
took weeks to heal. The swollen knuckle

reminds me that at 2 am that night, I had
no desire to reach for you.

Ode to experience

Love made me tentative, inarticulate, expectant, fearful and courageous.
Love made me demented, fragile, broken, and ashamed of being naïve.
Love made me selfless and whole, made me shine like polished silver.
Love made me realise that silver tarnishes.
Love made me self reliant and resilient, pragmatic and philosophical.
Love made me a good enough mother.
Love made me wary of men who say their wives don't understand them—
all the *separate bedroom* scenarios.
Love made me choosy.
Love made me appreciate polyamory on an intellectual level.
Love made me put on my polyarmoury.
Love made me unworried about love.
Love made me fill my life with poets and artists, academics and anarchists.
Love made me look to the wild, timbered hills and wander there.
Love made me, unmade me, and remade me.

How I love

Sometimes I say, *I love you, darling,*
and mean it. For friends, I prepare
a meal, choose fresh, organic ...

focus on the cutting, dicing, peeling
stir and simmer with my mind
bent towards perfection.

Meanwhile, I overlay the table
with a linen cloth. Its matching
serviettes—well-ironed triangles—lie

beneath inherited silver. Pre-loved
wine glasses—grape and vine embossed—
sit beside plain ones, for water.

In high school I learnt 'presentation'
so small, in-season flowers decorate my table.
In winter, a fire burns in the hearth.

In summer, a breeze wafts
through an open window. I make sure
each person shares the conversation.

Friends are not allowed to help clear up
or wash the dishes. I like to share that task
with my lover.

Schema

I grew up with sheep dung
and poetry, goannas in trees,
a pianola in the best room.

Guns and blood were as common
as church on Sunday.

Loving relatives and friends
were plentiful enough.

A man upset
my trajectory,
briefly.

I raised a child
with the help
of two suburbs.

Now I live alone in a house
I paid for and sometimes write
a poem after walking
in nearby bush, amazed,
as always, by its beauty
and my place
in the dwindling
scheme of things.

The twilight zone

im Janet Elizabeth Millar

Australia is losing

its frogs and bats.

Now we have

also to live with

the mental load

of losing *her.*

> Arum lilies wilt in a black vase, their flaccid stamens spent;
a crowd of scabbed peaches slouch on a chipped Kosta Boda dish;
a cockroach snacks on the breast of a quail dressed in fig leaves; smoke rises in
a thin eulogy for a candle burnt to its nubbin; Salvadore Dali's Melting Clock
reads midday or midnight; pearls spill from a broken strand abandoned on the
Noguchi coffee table, which leads the eye to the floor where a glass goblet lies
on its side; red wine seeps into the delicate pattern of the Afghan rug; a crone
sits in the corner, her wimple bent like her spine; a blowfly—there has to be
a blowfly—captured mid-air by the artist has an eerie iridescent green tinge
on its wings.

Some of my mother's maxims

On religion—
do unto others as you would have them
do unto you

On telling lies—
oh what a tangled web we weave
when first we practice to deceive

On opportunities lost—
that train
has left the station

On cry babies—
laugh and the world laughs with you;
cry and you cry alone

On domestic violence—
There are only two hits.
He hits you; you hit the road

On the big picture—
There is nothing wrong with the world,
only the people in it

My father chimes in—
There are more good people
in the world than bad

Dad, fifty years on, the trouble is
the few bad people have wealth,
power, and influence …

Cusp

We were thirteen, innocents
stumbling up polished stairs
to an empty public gallery—
our local court house.

We leant on the bannister,
looked down toward the bench,
elbowed each other, giggled,
at the wigged magistrate.

When we heard the charges,
we did not understand
the term, but as details
emerged, we stopped

giggling. My mouth
went dry. Body parts,
so far unnoticed, made
themselves known.

                              Later,

I asked my mother, *what is
carnal knowledge?* With
her usual candour, she told me.
A brutal reality I had not

thought possible, settled
in my pelvis. In another year,
dark blood stained my pyjamas.
A hatred of belts and pads

leached into monthly cycles.
I cursed the moon, my body,
three brothers asleep
in the backroom.

It would be another six
years before I encountered
carnality—another three
before I embraced it.

Family of origin

Dad ruled the roost

Mum feathered the nest

I flew the coop

Big tobacco

I'd read about
its tentacles
and techniques

for finding new
markets, how they
targeted the young,

people in the margins,
third and fourth
worlds, knowing

it's carcinogenic
properties maimed
and killed smokers.

I smoked thirty a day
in a windowless office,
inhaling deeply,

pictured two black lungs
fighting for air, even as I
lit the next cigarette.

It took three goes.
More determined
third time round,

I quit. It was the first
of many political acts
based on research.

Meaty bones

One of my father's professions—
tobacconist. He packed
the shelves of his barbershop

with every brand of cigarette,
tobacco, pipes, lighters …
smoked Benson & Hedges.

He moved my copy of a book
on big tobacco from the counter
to a drawer beneath the cash

register. Mum, open to data
and arguments, quit, but it took
a cardiologist to convince Dad

to stop smoking. It was just
one more bone of contention
we liked to chew.

O, how we loved those meaty bones!

Things I couldn't throw into the skip

Their wedding telegrams
His scout's badge and Jamboree Songbook
Her Girls Own Almanac, 1938

Their broken bedroom barometer
    (red and green arrows missing)
His framed business registration
Her workplace training program
    (*Transactional Analysis for Managers*)

Their mortgage discharge papers
His first pilots' licence
Her golf clubs

Their Morris Oxford Owners Manual
His plastic sandals
    (for fishing, Burrendong Dam)
Her paints and brushes, easels

His father's cutthroat razor, the strop
Her book of Scottish psalms
The receipt for their burial plots.

Comfort, Christmas 2020

Wanting comfort from home to take
to a Manhattan winter, my daughter
chooses a black and white dot painting.

'What's the story?' she asks.

You've picked a good one. The artist is kin—
a sister-in-law, elder and cultural leader
who knows all the stories, songs and dances.

When Nampitjinpa dotted the canvas with a stick,
I watched her hum and sing the story
as she worked—she told me how the women

gathered seeds, ground them on stone, cooked
damper on coals. The cake fed her family.
It's a fertility story as old as time. See the damage

on that edge? I don't know if it's black tea
or dog's piss, but the red dirt on the borders?
That's her country, where we sat together.

My daughter turns the painting over.
Nampitjinpa's name is written there,
with these words:

      BUSH SEED USED TO MAKE DAMPER
      ROADS TO COLLECT THEM

and her birth date, so close to mine.

She had trouble at the time—a granddaughter
had run away from boarding school; a brother,
stuck in Mt Isa, broke. I paid more than she asked

so she could travel along those roads. These days
bush seed battles it out with buffel grass and broken
glass. The painting is a celebration and lament.

She runs her fingers across the gritty edges,
says, 'I'll hang it above the kitchen table, think
of you and Nampitjinpa, bush seed, and bread."

PART 4

To the tourists who like to dress termite mounds

Maybe forty years ago, when the first drunken bum
stumbled off the Stuart Highway to dress a termite mound,
someone laughed.

Today, no one likes the way you remove your dirty tee-shirts,
your sweaty football guernseys, your underpants, to dress
the mounds.

Your girlfriend's broken underwire bras?
Surplus to requirements!

No lifeless models in a second-hand shop, these mounds
are cities made of spinifex, shit and spit, with sophisticated
air-conditioners—lungs that pump air

into a universe underground at even temperatures, elaborate
homes with galleries, tunnels, chambers, and throne rooms
for termite royalty,

complete with sewage farms and food stores, ensuring
sustenance for eggs and nymphs, keeping armies on the march
cleaning up the arid zone.

Water stories

We speak in plain English,
ask countrymen to share their stories,
changes they see.

Jangala begins—

> *I want to tell you a little story about the rain.*
> *Long time ago, we go, we go along rockholes*
> *and soakages. No water anywhere. All gone.*
> *That night, the old men—rainmakers—*
> *go way out, they sing and dance. We see*
> *a cloud coming up and think it's going to rain.*
> *Sure enough, rain comes down later that night.*
> *All the soakages and rockholes fill up. Only*
> *a few rainmakers left now …*

We wonder how
news of fracking
will go down.

Like rain seeping
into rockholes,
soakages,
the news
sinks
in.

Reflections from the riparian zone

1. Stockyard Creek - 1958

A grassy bank
string knotted
around a chunk
of meat dangled

Me and Aunty
Marg haul in
half a bucket
of yabbies we
cook and eat
Bellies full
we lie on
a grassy bank
look up,

interpret shapes
in clouds—
there's a rabbit,
says little I.
Aunty replies,
We'll have to trap it.

2. Cudgegong River 1—1960

Dressed in green speedos,
blowing a party whistle,
this discoloured photo

me—birthday girl—

aged ten, a picnic
by the river with Aunty
Mavis and her girls.

Where are my brothers?

Where is my father?

3. Cudgegong River 2—1971

In the park at midnight,
the windows of the car
misty with our kisses.

A policeman who knows
my father knocks on the
bonnet, tells us to move on.

4. Kemp Welch River, PNG—1974

The chaplain's wife and I lead an excursion—
Duke of Edinburgh Award, bronze and silver
medals. Students—teenage village girls—
show us how to make a raft, travel
on crocodile infested water.

We show them how to make
doughboys on a stick, filled
with golden syrup.

5. Lagaip River, PNG—1976

They cross the river twice a week—six girls, Grade 7 students—to
cook and sew with me. There is no female teacher. The headmaster
shows me how to write a lesson plan, hands me the curriculum. The
pay is *local,* the equivalent of thirty dollars a fortnight.

We locate three treadle sewing machines, set them up in my spare
bedroom, buy bobbins, cottons, one primus, then another.

On market days, the girls and I work out a budget, buy local produce
with a small allowance from the Board of Governors. Returning
home, we cook a meal using primuses and my wood stove.

On the front verandah, we eat what we have cooked, watch men from
the calaboose do time—hoe river flats, plant local crops for market,
potatoes expatriates will buy at the nearby Samu Trade Store.

At year's end, students get a proper teacher; I head south to Teachers'
College.

6. Ambum River, PNG—1980

After rain
the river
breaks
its banks
swallows
landslides
uproots
she-oaks
devours
the road
to town

We stand
well back
in awe
cut off
glad of
tinned
produce
our wood
heap, our
garden
and each
other

7. Lhere Mparntwe (Todd River)—1990

Folklore—if you see the river flow
three times you'll become a local; if
you leave you will return. Zero flow
for most of the year, visitors camp
beneath its ancient gums.

Some people wander to the tavern's
outside bar, drink in the sandy riverbed
or beneath its bridges. Young white men
in four-wheel drives practice circle work
at night. Vandals break and scatter glass,
set fire to sacred trees.

Women like me admire the river's beauty
from moving vehicles or the safety
of footbridges in broad daylight.

I return each year.

8. Molonglo River—1995

Perennial stream, bless your
Murrumbidgee confluence
near Uriarra Crossing,
your contribution to the
Murray-Darling Basin,
your tributaries and reserves,
your wetlands, dam and lake.
You have been our play-
ground, our swimming hole,

our paddling place, our water
source, for twenty-five years.

Perennial stream, bless
you for every one of sixty
thousand years you've shared
with Aboriginal clans.

9. Lander River—2013

Dry when I arrive, we cross on sand
engaged in four-wheel drive, meander
up the river's bank dropping off supplies—
blankets, bottled water, powdered milk,
flour, sugar, keep frozen tails of kangaroos
for those closest to the man who's died.

We all speak softly, words of comfort,
respectful of mourners' muted songs
of sorrow, their bowed, shaven heads …
Flowing swiftly when I leave, we cross
the river's tributaries many times, engaged
again in four-wheel drive. In the seat
beside me, gifts: a coolamon and digging
stick dotted blue and pink; a necklace
made of gumnuts painted red and black;
a canvas—bush potato dreaming—
Kaye has painted in her usual palette—
mementos of all our to and fro.

10. The Barka ('darling')—2018

Cotton upstream—
stagnant pools
unused wharf
no steamers
no fish

11. The Barkly—2020

When I lived here in the late eighties, this body of water was called
Mary Ann Dam. Today the local council have renamed it Lake Mary
Ann, given it a Warumungu name—*Tingkkarli*—but the sign does not
give its meaning.
I ask a Warumungu friend.
'It has no meaning—it's simply a women's dreaming place', a place she
feels at home.

12. Roper River—2021

On a riverbank with a sheer, two-metre drop, I sit with knowing
women. Pandanus and weeping paperbark branches dip their leaves
where turtles feed unseen. I'm nervous. Crocodiles. Salties. Unlikely
to climb this embankment, but if they do, will I have time to roll to
one side, run between the blackened trunks of the fan palms to the
unlocked four-wheel drive?

Any calm is troubled by my conscience. I have colonised Janie's
groundsheet, her fishing spot. She's moved down river leaving me
dangling a worried line. I catch nothing except my wan reflection.

Janie catches three turtles.

Too shy to ask, embarrassed by my earlier *faux pas*, I hang back. If the cooked flesh is offered I will taste it.

Janie teaches her daughter how to prize the flesh from the shell with a blunt knife, observe the protocols. Janie eats the liver—the sweetest delicacy. It is, after all, *her* catch.

Sam tells me turtle flesh tastes like chicken.

13. Water Lily Lagoon, 2022

Like the first pastoralists
we placed on a timeline
before this excursion,
our arrival disturbs …

magpie geese take flight
in awkward succession;
women collecting lotus
bulbs disappear into
savannah scrub in
elegant slow motion.

14. Top End 2022

Big rains

Big plans for cotton

Bigger water allocations for

Big white men

Big mistake

On Arrernte land in a stranger's house

Out there—on open country
working with traditional custodians—the horizon
generates feelings of generosity, possibility,
freedom.

Here, in a stranger's house,
corralled by corrugated iron fences
and a dull, tinfoil sky

the framed view from his window adds to the melancholia
I feel about flying south tomorrow. Waiting there—
a newly-purchased townhouse left unmade,

bought in the name of *downsizing*. Already I feel pinched
by apartment complex living—a body corporate,
common stairwells …

the imagined wintery vista—snow on the Brindabellas,
deciduous trees laid bare,
empty bee hotels …

slimmer than when I left, better in the gut, I have been freed
by good work on country, a course of neuro-probiotics,
his silence.

O! How I dread captivity.

Self portrait, February 2020

dedicated to the kookaburra

Refugee from bushfire,
smoke and storm—
will mincemeat do?
Sorry for your loss
of habitat. Thanks
for dropping in.
I don't blame you
for not eating from
my open hand.
On this day
of absences, will
you laugh for
a woman thinking
of the dead?

No matter, old love.

Lockdown

Alone, I walk O'Connor Ridge, its nearby
mountain, alternating steep with even trails.

If I've remembered to use my inhaler, I will
go up, up, up for city views. Otherwise,

I will wander towards the glistening pool.
With even breath, I'll sit a while, listen

to the frogs or watch the dragonflies dip
and drink. If the breeze picks up, I will

photograph the surface of the water,
try to capture how shapely reflections—

clouds and trees—disperse. Before this
contagion, would I have noticed frogspawn

in the rushes? Today, its presence seems
to sing an aria of hope, helps me hold on,

keeps me walking up a mountain, along
the ridge, noticing nearly everything.

Postcard from Bondi, 3 January 2021

Apartment blocks around here are named *Avoca,*

St Albans, Cranbrook; businesses called *Big John's*

Grill, Sasha's Hair, and *Kevin's Barbershop* do a slow

trade. *Pasha's Indian Restaurant* is closed for good,

its windows curtained in last year's tabloids.

In a nearby side street, a hoarder's front yard attracts

flies, pigeons and feral cats. Ancient paths are masked

by concrete, sandstone steps, and guardrails; middens

cloaked in bitumen. The view from our holiday house

is superb. We can see the curved beach, storms coming

in from every direction.

PART 5

Regent theatres, empire halls

Our generation imitated what we saw
at matinees on Saturdays. In backyards
we dressed up like cowboys, Indians,
pretended to be every hero John Wayne
played, donned feather headdresses to star
as Crazy Horse or Pocahontas in battles
fought at Little Bighorn. We smoked
peace pipes, used groundsheets to make
tepees, built forts, conflated histories.
We knew of tribes called Cherokee,
Comanche, Sioux, and Navajo. Ignorant
of Australia's recent past, we had never
heard of Koori or Wiradjiri, but *Abo*
had currency in our schoolyard.

In country towns in New South Wales
the Greeks ran cafes, Poles mended shoes,
the Germans rose to be more successful
than the landed gentry. Their children
went to school with us 'real Australians'.
A dark-skinned kid called Darkie said
he came from Pakistan. The Blackman
sisters reckoned they descended from
Kings and Queens in Tonga. Together
we learnt English history, paired up
and danced in empire halls. Puberty,
the '67 referendum, land rights demon-
strations, saw Darkie and the Blackman
girls remake history, build an Embassy.

Documentary, 1950

In children's lives, shrinking was the norm. Parents were poor
in post-war country towns, and grateful to be alive. Their hopes

were high, but hate was fresh as new laid eggs. Traumatised
ex-servicemen passed their trauma on. Their young sheltered

in innocent gangs like ringlets. Some unravelled in unruly
tendrils, meeting at weirs, in timbered hills behind a rifle range

or decommissioned brickworks, abattoirs. When swimming
pools were built, they spent summers diving for dark pebbles.

Their skin turned brown. They returned to fractured
fibro homes. Sometimes they hid in woodsheds. Timetables,

lists and rain gauge measurements were as important as the
Bible. Every penny counted. At school, children drank free

bottled milk warmed in morning sun, despite gagging. They
marched to military bands on quadrangles and playgrounds

in school uniforms, activities said to instil the order and precision
required for life itself. Relatives aplenty lived close by. Children

called in for cordial, patty cakes baked in fuel stoves, seeking
succour from sympathetic aunties. Saturday matinees conjured

accents from foreign English-speaking countries—drawl of
lasso, cuss of six-guns. In the darkness of picture theatres, they

could not see themselves. At racecourses, courthouses, saleyards,
men with mallets and megaphones adjudicated right from wrong,

price per pound, and winners. Radio stations had two announcers—
one for music, the other for local news and funeral notices.

To hear them, elders *shushed* the young. If familiar, the family
of the dead were given casseroles or cards were sent extending

sympathy in black ink. For many, time and place were fixed. Others
chased ideas in circles or found asylum in laps on rocking chairs.

When grown ups pricked balloons with toothpicks, a few courageous
souls took a pickaxe to thin air, ventured through low-lying cloud

to where horizons widened, and fences disappeared.

Afterword

In the five years since *Inlandia* (Recent Work Press), was published, several matters have exercised my pen.

Pre- and post-covid, good work in the Northern Territory with traditional custodians in two different sites has kept me grounded and engaged with teams I respect and learn from. Many poems centre on this work and associated experiences that have sustained me for the last forty years. It is always a privilege to be on country with people deeply connected to it, eager to share their knowledge in projects that they see as important and beneficial, and contribute to their success.

Terrifying climate change events and the global pandemic have fundamentally changed us. Sexual misbehaviour generally, and in our parliament by those elected to govern, continues to dismay us. The death of a good friend has made me reflect on loss and ageing in some poems. Others celebrate my relationships and the importance of engaging with the natural environment.

In the process of completing a Masters by Research on white privilege and its legacy in Australia at the University of Canberra, I was fortunate to be part of a field trip to Bourke and Brewarrina, places I had not visited before. I was also grateful to be a participant in *Story Ground* facilitated by Barkindji poet/writer, Paul Collis, a no-bullshit person I consider a friend.

As for the *Uluru Statement from the Heart*, what I like about the activites that lead to *Voice, Treaty, Truth* is that it used a bottom-up process, gained consensus by a majority of Indigenous peoples involved from across Australia

I will vote YES for constitutional recognition and *The Voice*. I worked in the Aboriginal and Torres Strait Islander Commission, a *legislative* body, one of many that have come and gone over the past fifty years, eliminated by the stoke of a pen wielded by a white male politician. That won't happen if *The Voice* is enshrined in the constitution. A YES vote is an opportunity for positive change. An opportunity for constitutional recognition is an opportunity for Aboriginal and Torres

Strait Islander voices to be raised in parliament on issues affecting them. It is an opportunity for non-Indigenous politicians to listen. It's a platform for *Treaty* and *Truth* to be progressed in the future. It is good to have Indigenous parliamentarians, but they are party-political.

This is a generous, but modest, invitation by First Nations people to the rest of us. If we are to heal this damaged nation, a YES vote is a vital first step.

Notes

p 3   Walker, Kath (Oodgeroo Noonuccal), *My People,* Jackaranda Press Pty Ltd, Melbourne, 1970. *Song of Hope* is on page 40 of this edition.

p 11   Emily Kame Kngwarreye (artist from Utopia, Northern Territory)

tjuringa (men's sacred object)

p 14   Jangala is one of eight Warlpiri skin names in their kinship system (men's side)

p 24   The Barkindji guide led us to and explained rock art in Gundabooka National Park, near Bourke. In Brewarrina, the fish traps were extraordinary.

p 33   Some lines in this poem are inspired by Tess Lea's book, *Wild Policy*

APS Australian Public Service

KPIs Key Performance Indicators

p 43   DSM The Diagnostic and Statistical Manual of Mental Disorders

p 45   The first manned moon landing occurred in 1969.

p 46   Stephanie Wood's book, *Fake,* details a time in her life when she was involved with a liar and fabulist. In this poem I mention yo-yo moves: *a sleeper; around the world; walking the dog.*

Acknowledgments

All hail to the usual subjects and the generous poetry community in Canberra.

Janet Millar and my daughter, Noni, were first readers of many poems in this collection. They provided critical insights or reassurance on draft poems. Family and friends have read and approved of poems about them.

Between 2020 and 2023, my supportive poetry group relocated and changed its name twice, then learnt how to Zoom. For their perseverance, feedback and friendship I thank: Moya Pacy, Sandra Renew, Rosa O'Kane, Hazel Hall and Sue Peachey.

Poetry weekends at *Geebung*, facilitated by Nicola Bowery and Harry Laing, have been important in keeping my creativity alive. I have benefitted from participating in their stimulating workshops, their introduction to the work of a wide range of international and local poets, and their invitation to read at Stanley Street Gallery.

The annual Poetry on the Move Festival organised by the University of Canberra has sustained me in hard times.

Other invitations to read have come from Geoff Page, Manning Clark House, That Poetry Thing That Is On At Smith's Every Monday, and Not Very Quiet. I ran poetry workshops at the Tuggeranong Art Centre and the Burra Regional Art Gallery (as part of their exhibition, *Here, There & Everywhere: Cait Wait and the Warraweena Artists)*. Thank you all!

To the directors, staff and fellow associates of Centrefarm Aboriginal Horticulture Limited; the directors, members and traditional custodians of Alekarenge Horticulture Pty Ltd; the Mungarrayi and Wubaluwun traditional custodians; and the Lander River Nampijinpas: your knowledge, friendship, generosity and humour continues to sustain and inspire me.

To the Tennant Creek Mob Aboriginal Corporation: your wonderful work with the Warumungu and Tennant Creek community demonstrate how well bottom-up processes work for the benefit of the *whole* community.

I thank everyone who has published my work.

To my editor, Penelope Layland: thank you for your patience, generosity and feedback. Your encouragement to 'dig deeper' strengthened this collection.

Last but not least, to my publisher, Shane Strange of Recent Work Press: where would I/we be without you?

Several poems in this collection have been previously published in the ACU Prize for Poetry, *Hope; Arena,* the Old Water Rat Publishing e-journal, *Burrow; Canberra Times;* Newcastle Poetry Prize Anthology, *Buying Online;* Newcastle Writers' Centre, *Grieve;* the online women's poetry journal, *Not Very Quiet; Not Very Quiet: the Anthology; Poetry d'Amour;* and *Rabbit Poetry Journal.*

K A Nelson is a country girl whose destiny—marriage/children—was thwarted by her love of difference and the opportunity to travel and work in New Zealand, Papua New Guinea, Italy, Central Australia and elsewhere. Prime Minister Gough Whitlam assisted her desire to learn by paying her a small allowance to attend Sydney Teachers' College in 1977-78 and the University of New England in 1982-84. Treasurer and Prime Minister Paul Keating contributed to her financial independence with his government's superannuation policies.

Between 2016 and 2020 K A Nelson studied a Masters by Research at the University of Canberra. Her exegesis and memoir with poetry focused on white privilege and its legacy in Australia together with lessons learnt from her working life with Aboriginal and Torres Strait Islander peoples in rural, regional and urban settings between 1981-2020.

Since 2011 Centrefarm Aboriginal Horticulture Limited has engaged her as a two-way governance facilitator, educational associate, and team member in an innovative mapping project with traditional custodians. She hopes this important work continues and that her body holds up so she can continue to be involved.

As always, her greatest achievement and joy has been raising her daughter to independent adulthood with lots of love and community development principles.